simple outdoor style

simple

outdoor

◆ style ◆

LJILJANA BAIRD

Photographs by Olivier Maynard

M·Q·P

Acknowledgements

Many, many thanks to Malabar for generously providing fabrics for the projects
and to Susan Marfleet for her swift and efficient despatch of last minute fabric requests.
Thanks also to Tricia Tucker and her team for realising the design sketches.

Published by MQ Publications, Ltd.
254-258 Goswell Road, London EC1V 7EB

Copyright © MQ Publications, Ltd. 1998

Text © Ljiljana Baird 1998
Photographs © Olivier Maynard 1998

Series Editor: Ljiljana Baird
Editor: Simona Hill
Designer: Bet Ayer

1 3 5 7 9 8 6 4 2

A CIP catalogue record for this book is available from the British Library

ISBN: 1 897954 13 1

Printed in Italy

contents

◆

introduction

◆

Mention the word outdoor and we conjure up images of hiking across the countryside, camping in woods and forests, boating on lakes and rivers and swimming and sailing on the sea. It suggests fresh air and space to be oneself. Outdoors can also encompass situations more domestic and closer to home – the local park, your own garden and even a patio or balcony for those of us who live in apartments in a city environment. The outdoors carries notions of well-being, relaxation, challenging recreational activities and places that are free from day to day pressures.

The outdoors offers physical and emotional escape from the enclosures and boundaries which prescribe our activities and behaviour, whether we be at home, school, or our workplace. I have always regarded it as the great release – the 'breathe out'. Watch children tumble out of class into the playground or from a bus on an outing – they squeal and roar and run with pleasure at the freedom. Even when our normal daily activities are happy and smooth-running, the outdoors offers a welcome recreational and relaxing change. But when life makes too many demands and we are desperate for relief from daily pressures, many of us like to take a brisk walk, work in the garden or collapse on a beach. In short, we distance ourselves physically from the pressure points and, in doing so, claw back a little space in which to assess and review our problems. The old-fashion remedy of stepping-out to take the air is not dissimilar to current medical advice for healthy living –

take plenty of fresh air and exercise. The fresh air blows the cobwebs away and encourages activities of a type that are usually enjoyable and the fun element in turn helps to relieve stress and the accompanying unattractive physical symptoms of our fast-track lifestyle.

The outdoors is a vital ingredient in a happy and healthy life. *Simple Style Outdoors* looks at projects that can enhance our enjoyment of this wonderful natural resource in the spring and summer months. Outdoor activities can be marred by too much sun and wind, irritating insects, uncomfortable seating and inappropriate tableware.

The criteria put to each project for inclusion in the book were – simplicity of design and construction, function, safety, attractiveness, ease of maintenance, portability, availability and economy of materials. When a project answered positively to all these requirements then it was included. A simple lifestyle is essentially about an easy, low maintenance way of living, from which fuss and extraneous knick knacks are removed to optimise time and space for the priorities. But at the same time as paring back, simple style is observant of the visual appeal of what remains. We want to surround ourselves with objects in which function and style work together as one. With these objectives in mind simple style still remains a personal approach. Each reader will interpret the suggestions and guidelines within their own set of preferences and adapt the projects to best suit themselves.

The book is divided into five categories that roughly address the main aspects of domestic outdoor life – lounging, shade and shelter, eating, seating and accessories. The projects have been designed in the simplest possible way to ensure that they are within every reader's making capabilities, using equipment, tools and materials that can be found in their local DIY or department store. Making-up time and cost were also important considerations. Outdoor furniture and accessories must be reasonably robust to withstand the demands of the elements and our general neglect. Most of us are reluctant to pack away at the first indication of wet weather, items get left out, and within a few seasons, materials and fabrics perish. So if we are to replace or refurbish outdoor equipment, speed of construction should be considered. Re-covering a deck chair or the folding picnic stools requires less than an hour's work; a set of six button tablemats can be sewn in a few hours; similarly the container

candles, the envelope cushion and hammock can be made in a morning. Because I know that to replace any of projects will not demand much of my time, I can relax about leaving them outside in wind and weather. Not being anxious about one's possessions is an important factor in a simple lifestyle. I am not suggesting that we are neglectful; rather I'm suggesting that with better planning and forethought about what we buy or make for our home, we can reduce our maintenance worries without sacrificing appearance. For example, you want the peace of mind that, should a guest spill drink or food on a tablecloth, chair covering or cushion, or children drop ice cream on the hammock, that the offending blemish can be simply removed by a quick wash in the machine. So for convenience, choose fabrics that are readily available, inexpensive and easily cleaned. For all the sewn projects I have chosen natural fibres such as cotton and linen. These are ideal fabrics for the outdoors – they are available in a wide range of standard and fashion colours, they are machine washable, they press well and hang beautifully and they are easy to handle when making up. Being comfortable to the skin, they are especially suitable for hot weather and, unlike polyester- and nylon-based fabrics, do not as a rule cause skin irritation. These two fabrics also look good – natural-coloured or bleached linen or cotton are elegant. They are

sympathetic and blend with the
beige striped cotton fabric looks
colours of a summer garden and
beach, or against the greens of
jects I have selected outrageously
with nature's own exuberant
pink, madras cotton director's
colourful herbaceous border.
pink with lime green in a patch-
fun of outdoor living, as do
chosen for the two-coloured

colours of the outdoors. Beige-on-
wonderful against the riotous
would look equally well on a
trees. In contrast, for other pro-
bright colours in competition
summer palette. The candy
chair cover sings as loudly as a
Combining squares of orange and
work picnic cloth expresses the
the orange and yellow colours
tablecloth and matching chair.

Like bees we are attracted by colour – it lifts our spirits and provides nourishment of sorts.

I have avoided patterned fabrics, choosing for the projects solids or stripes, and in one instance a plaid. Patterns date, whereas classic stripes and plaids remain timeless and unobtrusive. They are also much easier to mix and match. Patterned fabrics are frequently too busy and distract from the function of the item. When thinking about your table linen, consider the colour of your china and glassware; they need to enhance each other. I think the yellow wine glasses look superb against the natural-coloured linen of the beaded tablerunners on page 60 – the colours invite you to the table and that is the function of a table setting.

As you create the props for your outdoor life, keep in mind the function of each object – that way you will ensure that your garden is full of furnishings that are are comfortable, practical and desirable. If function is your guide then attractiveness, and simplicity of design and style will follow.

INTRODUCTION

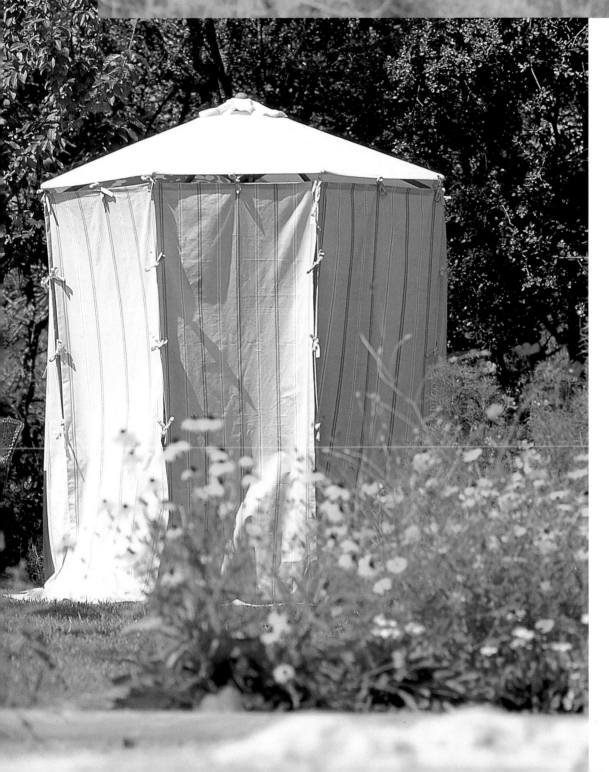

shade and shelter

T he past several years have seen a change in attitude to sunbathing and, while we are encouraged to use the outdoors as another living space, we have also been advised of the long-term ill effects of prolonged exposure to sunlight, not to mention the immediate discomfort of sunburn. But at the same time we want to be stylish, not be covered from head to toe, swamped in oversize tee-shirts and full-brimmed hats. Outdoors is about looking good but it is also about being comfortable and safe and having fun. To this end, this chapter offers four amazingly simple-to-make but stylish projects that provide shade and shelter and will appeal to everybody – a parasol tent quite large enough for a small tea party that doubles up as a private outdoor reading room or elegant poolside changing

booth; a beach awning suspended from long bamboo poles or which, in a woodland setting, can be tied to the branches of trees; a heavenly white voile canopy that protects against irritating insects, both indoors and outdoors and a windbreak-cum-outdoor shower screen, complete with storage pockets for newspapers, sun lotion, toothbrush and comb. I have chosen mainly neutral colours for all the projects to allow them to rest quietly, look good and blend in anywhere outdoors. All the projects are portable and are designed to be used at home in the garden, on the beach, in the woods, by the swimming pool, on the riverbank or in the park. For ease, choose fabrics and materials that are lightweight but strong and machine wash-

able. These include strong woven natural fabrics such as canvas, cotton cambric, calico, denim, chambray, ticking, drill, duck, khaki, oilcloth and sailcloth. They must be able to stand the rigours of repeated handling.

If an item is a permanent summer fixture choose neutral shades that will not fade in the sun, and pick fabrics strong enough to withstand the harshness of summer weather.

12 ◄

SHADE AND SHELTER

parasol
changing tent

◆

It was from watching my children fashion such successful and innovative 'homes' from everyday materials lying about that the idea of a campaign-type tent came to mind. On this occasion, it happened to be beach towels draped over an umbrella which happily accommodated two children, dolls and pets. A private hideaway, just for two, a tête-à-tête in the calm cool of the garden with the same ease of assembly appealed to me as well. In response I have come up with a design that requires no further skills than sewing a straight line. Using a sturdy white canvas market parasol, now a familiar sight on patios, balconies and gardens, as my structure, I simply attached eight panels of fabric to the rim of the umbrella. So that the tent can be brought in for the winter I have chosen the simplest of fasteners – rings and ties. The panels are tied through rings to the parasol and the panels are tied together down the length. This method also allows you to roll up panels as you wish for light and ventilation.

▶ 15

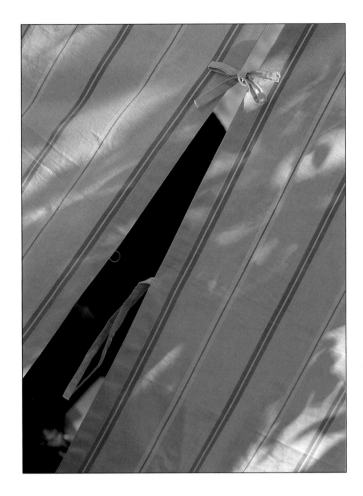

Ties and small brass rings make this tent easy to assemble and allow individual panels to be rolled up as desired.

voile
canopy

◆

Late afternoon and early evening – often the most pleasant and relaxing hours of a summer's day – can be ruined by the insects that come out to enjoy the balmy hours. A portable canopy, suspended from a rope or branch, is an excellent solution when midges and mosquitoes are troublesome.

As it made sense to be able to use the canopy indoors as well, I designed the shape to fit over a standard single bed giving me plenty of fabric to fit over an outdoor summer bed or reclining chair. The canopy is made from four pieces of delicate white cotton voile – a single panel which hangs behind the bed, a long rectangular panel that runs diagonally from the point of suspension to the floor and two triangular side panels. The net is hung from a band of looped tabs the width of the back panel.

beach
awning

◆

An all-day outing in full sunshine on the beach can benefit from a good source of shade. Unlike a standard sun umbrella, this awning can accommodate a family and all the trappings of an outing. The rectangular shape marks out your territory for the day and provides a camp – somewhere to unload, spread out a picnic, take a nap, read a book and, for the children, somewhere to play out of the sun.

The design and construction could not be easier – lengths of fabric have been machine stitched to make up the size and eyelets have been punched into the four corners. The guy ropes are threaded through the eyelets and lashed to long bamboo poles which are easily fixed into the sand. On a riverbank or in the woods, dispense with the poles and simply fix hammock-wise to four sturdy branches.

windbreak

◆

The times I have been lured outside by a bright sky only to find a cool breeze actively taking the heat out of the day are too numerous to mention. This is especially true on the beach, where sea breezes can quickly affect the mood of bathers! The old-fashion windbreak is just the answer – it excludes the interloper and enjoyment resumes.

The windbreak is made up of as many panels as you wish; usually there are three or four panels, sewn together with a long pocket between each panel for the supporting poles. Choose strong but lightweight fabrics. To withstand the wear, double stitch all seams using a heavy-duty sewing thread. I have avoided the obvious beach-side deck chair and awning stripes and have chosen solid colours of blues and greens and finished the top edge with a decorative row of large silver eyelets.

lounging

▶ 27

Relax, put your feet up is one of the stock principles of outdoor living. This chapter looks at four simple means of doing just that (in comfort) – the hammock, deck chair, floor cushion and beach mat.

For comfort use fabric that is soft and pleasing to the touch. For instance, re-cover your deck chair with a pre-washed canvas, cotton duck, or even linen. Lighter-weight cotton fabrics such as poplin and madras can also be used if lined. Do not use nylon fabric substitutes. Although they are available for this specific use and will not perish if left out in the rain, they are hot and sticky to sit on, especially with bare skin, and will make a hot summer's day even hotter. This advice holds true for all the projects. You need to feel comfortable to relax, which is why a wooden garden recliner, although attractive to the eye, gets short shrift when competing with anything like a hammock or deck chair with foot rest and canopy.

The four projects in this chapter can be made very economically both in time and money, so the items do not have to be dragged in at first sight of inclement weather for fear of damage. They can be replaced easily. Re-covering a deck chair with canvas can be done for less than ten pounds. Be on the

lookout for old deck chairs to renovate. Often old frames are more interesting in line than new ones, and, if you are really lucky, you might even find one with foot rest and canopy. I picked up the chair on page 35 for three pounds, removed the nylon decking, stripped away the pale blue paint to reveal the natural colour of the pine wood and re-covered it with new canvas. The process took less than three hours.

LOUNGING

hammock

◆

A hammock strung between two leafy trees is the epitome of relaxation in the outdoors. It has so many happy and romantic associations – the Mediteranean siesta or the castaway on a desert island. It truly does represent the easy life. Everyone is happy to idle away some time in the embrace of a hammock and be transported by the breeze, the hum of bees and the perfume of the trees to their own desert island. A hammock is easy to make – it is quite simply a length of wood with a dozen holes drilled into it at regular intervals with some sturdy rope threaded through eyelets in a length of strong fabric – the colour and pattern to your own taste. To make the hammock clews, you can use either natural or synthetic strings. Natural strings are more attractive, softer and easier to work with. Synthetic strings on the other hand are stronger and will not perish when left outdoors.

▶ 31

deck chair

◆

No summer is complete without at least one comedy routine of assembling a deck chair and I suspect that we have all enjoyed a laugh at somebody else's expense as they frantically fashion each new and fantastic shape. The practicality and comfort of deck chairs makes them well worth the occasional assembly hiccup. They fold flat and are wonderfully easy to store over the winter months, and their simple and robust design guarantee a long life. Unless subject to long bouts of wind and rain a quality deck chair will last a long time. The only aspect needing attention is the canvas, which may need replacing after two or three seasons, if only for cosmetic reasons. The decking is easily replaced and requires no more than a handful of tacks and a length of canvas which you can buy in ready-cut deck-chair lengths from most good fabric suppliers.

▶ 35

LOUNGING

beach mat
and bag

◆

This neat double act is a must for all those sun wor-
shippers and sunbathers who do not relish the
thought of lugging furniture across the dunes but who,
at the same time, want more comfort than is provided
by a towel. The beach mat is simply a 2.5–5cm/
1–2in thick piece of super-light foam covered with a
removable seersucker sleeve. For portability, it rolls
up easily to fit into a matching duffel bag. Rolled up it
makes for a very comfortable head rest. For the cas-
ing choose a soft cotton fabric that is comfortable to
the skin and that washes well at high temperatures. I
chose seersucker, which comes in a good selection
of bright and cheerful colours; other suitable fabrics
are percale, madras and chambray.

To give a maritime touch to the ensemble, use a thick, all-cotton cord for the drawstring. Drawn tight it makes an attractive and decorative collar. Add a pocket to the outside of the bag to store your sun lotion and other small personal effects.

floor
cushion

◆

Cushions are an attractive addition to one's comfort and the larger they are, the more inviting they become. An outsize cushion on a rug under a shady tree is an ideal spot for escaping to with a good book. By its nature, a floor cushion should be designed for a fair amount of wear and tear without forsaking appearance. This 'window' design cushion is made using a sky-blue linen and cotton union with a zip fastener at the bottom for easy maintenance. It is simply decorated with two squares of contrasting-coloured fabric applied with a chunky-look blanket stitch.

LOUNGING

accessories

▶ 43

Accessories are those decorative items that we can do without but are better off for having – the icing on the cake, as it were. There are so many possible projects that could have been included in this chapter – birdhouses, bird tables, planters, small furniture, a weather vane and water fountain are just some ideas that were considered. The four I finally chose sum up the elements that constitute simple style, namely – function and simplicity in design, materials and construction. Added to that, the design must be attractive and have a contemporary appeal. I also wanted projects that required no other skills than being able to follow a simple set of instruc-

tions. The lavender window box – is easy to make from materials that or have ready access to, and if you can be substituted with any other The hessian tote bag is another project materials – the hessian, although be obtained as sacking when buying of pebbled paving stones always first time visitors – "How wonderful;

an innovative recycling project – most of us have either in our garden don't have lavender stalks then they aromatic semi-hardwood plant. that could make use of recycled available to buy off the bolt, can also animal feeds. The sight of a path generates the same response from I want to make some". Made of

such a humble everyday work material, these decorated concrete slabs seem to liberate the artist/craftsperson in all of us. The final project in this chapter is making container candles. They are an attractive simple-to-make alternative to standard outdoor lighting and have endless scope. You can fill jam jars, yoghurt pots, drinking glasses and vases; you can use frosted glass and coloured glass. Apart from glass there are pottery and ceramic containers as well as metal and heavy duty plastics. Besides the obvious romance candlelight offers, container candles are an effective non-toxic insect deterrent that can be perfumed with your favourite scents.

lavender
flower box

◆

Each year at the end of summer when I trim back the lavender, I set about thinking what I can do with all the stalks. I've made the obvious – sachets, pot-pourri and I've hung bunches up to dry – but that only uses a fraction of the harvest. I longed for something truly resourceful that would make good use of what would otherwise be added to the garden compost. I came up with an idea for an aromatic window box, woven from lavender cuttings, which would last through the winter months as a reminder of summer. Using an existing window box as a base, I ran garden wire around it to make a mesh through which to weave the lavender. When I had built up a thick layer of stalks, I simply slid the base out, leaving a free-standing container which I lined with heavy-duty black polythene before planting up. This principle can be used to make boxes using other woody-stemmed herbs.

garden
candles

◆

Warm summer evenings beckon people outdoors for meals, conversation or just simply to watch the stars. But some form of lighting is necessary. Evening is a romantic and peaceful time, and the light we use should reflect its softness. There are any number of lighting fixtures available to us today, from electrical garden lights to small pin lights but the most beautiful and evocative without question are candles. Container candles are easy to make and, the selection of shape and size is as wide as the variety of containers. The collection on the page opposite includes an assortment of glassware found in the kitchen – drinking glasses, jam jars, plastic yoghurt pots and a large vase. By adding a drop of fragrance in wax you can keep the insects at bay ensuring a truly peaceful evening.

48 ◀

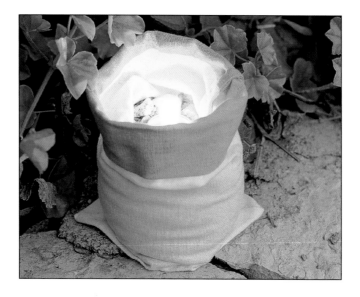

Small canvas bags filled with wet sand and a night light make wonderful low-level garden lights. Here they line the stone wall leading to the garden gate – perfect for outdoor parties.

hessian
tote bag

◆

I have made a concerted effort to avoid using the plastic carrier bag that has so invaded our lives. They have come to represent our buy-and-throw-away consumerism that is leaving a legacy of mountains and mountains of non-disposable plastic matter. I've made several of these easy-to-make tote bags using three of the most durable materials – hessian, ticking and webbing. These old-time workaday materials are sturdy and make a stylish but practical team. Lined with 100 percent cotton ticking the bag is a suitable shopping tote and an all-purpose carrier for garden cuttings and produce. Hung up in the shed, unlined versions make excellent storage for bulbs, small tools, gardening paraphernalia or dry pet foods.

▶ 51

pebble paving
stones

◆

Most of us are collectors and we all seem to have a need to bring our experiences home in some tangible form. Who can refrain from pocketing occasional souvenir shells or coloured beach glass, driftwood or smooth round pebbles. Over the years the collection grows until one day you are driven to ask yourself what to do with it all. Artist Wendy Wilbrahem knows exactly what do with the pebbles she collects – she integrates them into unusual pebble mosaics.

ACCESSORIES

Simplicity of material, design and construction sums up simple style and I felt the pebble paving stones project was perfect for this book. Wendy has designed a set of paving squares with a wandering floral motif that can be joined up in a linear fashion or into larger squares. Work out your design with just the pebbles on a square of paper before committing yourself to mixing the cement.

On the previous page is an example of a simple geometric design. The method of construction remains the same for whatever design you choose.

eating

▶ 57

E ating *al fresco* is one of the great pleasures of life, whether it be a family barbecue on the patio, a party, a picnic or a formal tea in the garden. It is a social activity which gives the occasion its vital ingredient – fun. At your next barbecue, stand back and observe for a moment – you will probably find everyone involved in the preparation – there's someone watching the barbecue, another cutting the bread, someone pouring drinks while others prepare salad or clean strawberries. And it is a very relaxed occasion, full of chatter.

A picnic basket of fairly average contents holds more excitement and enjoyment than the same items at the kitchen table. It is the ambience and the occasion that enhances the taste and look of food. The outdoors encourages people to relax – children and adults are free from the anxiety of spillage, and in truth, fewer accidents seem to happen outdoors. And if the rogue glass of wine should fall, the outdoors takes it in its stride simply absorbing the incident – unlike a carpet that demands immediate, panicky attention.

Eating outdoors encourages simpler menus. The ferrying of hot food outside is not very practical so dishes are adapted. We settle for more salads, fresh bread, barbecue grilled meats and vegetables, cheese platters and fruit, in fact an altogether healthy diet. It also means that the cook spends less time preparing and cooking meals and spends more time with the family or guests.

Table linen for the outdoors should be simple in design to maintain and reflect the casual mood of outdoor living. The four projects in this chapter cover all possible outdoor meals — simple mats for a family tea, linen tablerunners for a garden party, a colourful patchwork cloth for a picnic and a two-toned cloth for a more formal occasion.

EATING

beaded tablerunners

◆

These long, beaded runners are ideal to dress a large buffet table and can be made using any fabric. I chose a raw linen so that the colour of the food and the bright ceramic ware would look inviting to the guests. Find a colour and texture that looks good with your china; try to avoid fussy florals as these will draw attention away from the food.

To add interest and detail, the hems are finished with neat mitres and brought to the right side of the fabric. To emphasise the pendant effect of the runners I have added lines of small hand-carved wooden beads to the short sides. The beads are strung onto linen threads drawn from the same fabric and then the different length lines of beads are knotted into the hem. Select beads that closely match your chosen fabric. There is such a large variety of beads available from specialist stores that you should have no problem in finding a perfect match.

buttoned
tablemats

◆

These stripe-on-stripe tablemats are simply constructed from two rectangles of fabric – the smaller placed on the larger and secured with four dainty shell buttons at each corner, so easy, a full set can be machine-sewn in an afternoon. Using the same fabric design, make a set of different-coloured mats – one for each member of the family – and team up with plain-coloured napkins. The secret to co-ordinating many different colours is to make sure that all the colours are the same tone.

The design is pleasant and can be comfortably used for a summer's day lunch or as settings for a casual evening meal.

SIMPLE STYLE OUTDOORS

two-coloured tablecloth

◆

Decked in the bright warm colours of the Mediterranean, this table dressing is suitable for any meal time – formal or casual. It can be dressed up or down to suit the occasion. With such lively colours for the background, choose your china with care – liveliness from all corners makes for a very confused table. I chose rich brown Provencale earthenware to complement my two favourite colours. This cloth will be equally effective in any number of colour arrangements. My first thought was to choose a soft teal blue, offset with a delicate sea green, then the idea of musk pink and raspberry occupied my attention. Both ideas were abandoned when I visualised the cloth with my china. For comfort when seated around the table, and to avoid the familiar tangle of guest and cloth, I designed it with slits which start at floor level and finish almost at the table top.

patchwork
picnic cloth

◆

Large, effervescent pink and orange rectangles sur-
rounded with a bright lime green border are the elements that make up this eye-catching picnic cloth.
The simple design allows you to make it in any combination of colours. You may prefer a less hectic
palette or you may want to introduce some patterned
fabrics such as checks and ginghams to offset solid
colours; such combinations will work just as effective-
ly and give a more rustic appeal. Worked in large
scale, brightly-coloured florals are another alternative
for this design. This cloth is a great project for any
beginner – the shapes are big and easy to handle,
requiring only straight line seams and the embellish-
ment is a simple running stitch – an instant success!

seating

▶ 69

Make light work of your outdoor seating. All garden furniture cannot be left out of doors throughout the year: wooden chairs can be treated with preserving oils and varnish finishes and metal furniture can be painted or sealed, but furniture incorporating fabrics will perish. It can withstand occasional showers but is best put away during the winter months. Bearing in mind your storage facilities, choose

chairs that are lightweight and can be folded or stacked conveniently. Having a designated storage area also means that they can be put away quickly and easily if inclement weather persists.

The chairs in this chapter will most probably function as outdoor dining chairs, so they must provide a reasonable level of comfort and support – certainly sufficient to get through the length of a meal. So when choosing your chairs, try them for comfort and take into account the height of the table that will be used in conjunction with the chairs. For projects, I have chosen to dress chairs that I imagine most people

have – the ubiquitous director's chair, the common slatted garden chair and the all-purpose folding picnic stool which, although not suitable for a dinner, is an invaluable standby when extra seating is needed.

Avoid polyester and synthetic fabrics for seating – they are hot and sticky. You can pick up deck chair canvas, artist's canvas and cotton duck very cheaply from specialist art suppliers.

SEATING

envelope cushion covers

◆

It is hard to imagine a sewing project could be so easy. Two linen tea cloths and five buttons make up the materials list for this extremely stylish and practical cushion cover. There are many wonderful tea cloths available to buy, some patterned with checks or open grids, others with chequerboard designs or stripes. Conveniently, most are the exact width of a standard cushion pad. This means that you can utilise many of the woven border and trimming patterns in your cushion cover design. The only sewing required is stitching two cloths together to give sufficient length to wrap a cushion front and back with a generous flap and adding buttonholes.

The cover is sealed on the sides with two small buttons. For extra strength, you may want to sew a small length of tape to the sides before making the buttonholes.

covered chairback and seat

◆

Although attractive to look at, wooden garden chairs don't always provide the level of comfort that we would like and getting through the duration of a meal can be hard work. You can add cushion pads, but they slide off unless fastened to the chair, and in any case, that still leaves your back resting against the hard wooden slats. The chairback cover is a simple device of two rectangles of fabric with slightly tapered ends sandwiching a thick layer of wadding. The cover folds over the back and front of the chairback and is secured by tie fasteners on either side of the chair. Easy to remove for washing and storage, this cover idea is simple to make and is an effective way of transforming an obdurate chair.

SEATING

director's chair
loose cover

◆

Director's chairs provide a cheap and comfortable form of seating for outdoors. Lightweight and fold-away, they are ideal portable furniture.

The frames, usually made of wood with metal bracing, are quite sturdy and will last several seasons. The canvas back and seating, on the other hand, will probably need replacing, if only for cosmetic reasons. There are several types of director's chairs and the instructions given can be adapted to fit any type. Choose fabric colours and patterns that co-ordinate with other items of garden furniture. For easy mainte-nance, use only quality cotton fabrics that can be washed at high temperatures. I chose a colourful madras cotton for the chair cover opposite, while for the cover of the formal dining chair on page 68, I chose a crisp, white cotton and linen union.

folding
picnic stool

◆

Obviously ideal for away-from-home activities such as picnics and sporting fixtures where weight and portability are of concern, folding stools are also invaluable when additional seating is needed for a garden party. Although most guests are happy to stand, many will welcome a short respite off their feet, especially when trying to negotiate food, drink and conversation at the same time.

The canvas seating comprises a small rectangle of fabric, with channels on either side, which slide onto the metal frame. So simple to make, you can make a new set for any special occasion and paint the metal frame to match. To offset the bright pink and orange seating and give a contemporary look, I painted the frames with silver to give a galvanised silver finish.

putting it together

To make *Simple Style Outdoors* accessible to all readers, projects have been designed that employ the simplest and most obvious methods of construction. The non-sewing projects require a sprinkle of

common sense and the ability to follow some basic instructions. The sewing projects require no more than being able to sew a straight seam on the sewing machine. Although all items can be sewn by hand, for strength and durability and for ease of sewing, machine sewing is advisable.

The success of the projects depends largely on your choice of materials, the colours and the finish. Take time in choosing your materials and always buy what pleases you; try not to compromise because you'll only be dissatisfied with it further on down the line and then abandon it. Choose the best quality materials available. Although initially more

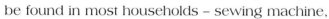

expensive, they will handle and wear better and stand the test of time.

All the projects have been made using natural products – 100 percent cotton or linen; sisal rope and bamboo for the beach awning cotton rope for the hammock clews, hessian for the tote bag. Natural products are usually easier to handle and often wear better. The exception is rope: nylon rope is stronger and will not perish.

The equipment needed for making any of the projects is basic and can

be found in most households – sewing machine, scissors and pins for the sewing projects; pliers and garden wire for the lavender box; saucepan and scales for the candles; and bucket and spade for the pebble paving stones. For projects using eyelets such as the hammock, beach awning and windbreak, eyelet-making kits are available to buy from haberdashery stores. If, however, you are using a particularly heavy fabric for any of these projects, take a sample swatch with you to the store to make certain that the kits available are suitable for your choice of fabric. If not, then have the eyelets punched in professionally. Most blind-making companies, awning manufacturers and upholsterers can provide this service.

PUTTING IT TOGETHER

parasol changing tent

◆

To adapt the panels to fit your parasol, measure the width of each parasol section and the height from the shade to the ground.

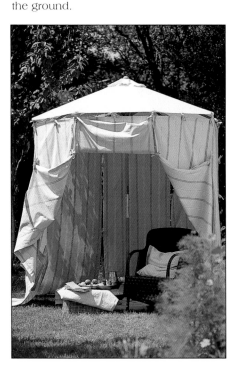

MATERIALS
◆ *Pre-purchased octagonal-shape parasol*
◆ *11m/12yd fabric to match*
◆ *Curtain rings – 40*
◆ *Sewing kit*

1 Cut eight panels 84 x 216cm/33 x 85in.

2 Press a 0.75cm/¼in seam all around. Turn in another 3cm/1¼in and press.

3 Mitre the corners: unfold the seams and turn in the corners. Clip the diagonal, leaving a small seam allowance. Turn in the seam. Refold the edges.

4 Press, then hand stitch the mitre.

5 To make the ties, cut 40 strips 5 x 56cm/2 x 22in. Turn in 1.5cm/½in at each short end. Press. Fold each strip in half lengthways. Press. Open out the fold. Turn in the raw edges to the centre fold. Refold, then stitch across each short end and down the long edge. *(see picture next column)*

6 Fold the tie in half and pin to the top right-hand corner of the wrong side of the panel. Add a second tie to the top centre. To the top left-hand side stitch a curtain ring. Stitch three ties at even intervals to the left-hand side of the panel. Stitch three curtain rings to correspond on the right-hand side.

7 Add rings to correspond with the ties.

beach awning

◆

This awning can be made up to any size and any height and almost any shape. Keep the poles and awning in proportion. Choose a sturdy all-cotton fabric or canvas that can withstand substantial wear and tear.

MATERIALS
◆ *3.2m/3 ½yd strong cotton fabric*
◆ *Eyelets*
◆ *Bamboo poles*
◆ *Rope*
◆ *Sewing kit*

1 Cut the fabric in half across the width and sew the two halves together along the length.

2 Turn under 5cm/2in at each edge and press. Turn under a further 5cm/2in and press again.

3 Double topstitch along all edges.

4 Following the manufacturer's instructions, insert one eyelet in each corner.

voile canopy

◆

This canopy is made up of four sections – a rectangle for the back, two right-angle triangles for the sides and one other rectangle for the front.

● Cut the largest pieces from the fabric first.

1 For the front panel, cut one length 328cm/129in.

2 At one short edge, for the bottom, turn in 0.75cm/¼in. Press. Turn in another 3.75cm/1½in. Press and stitch.

3 Turn in a double hem at each long side. Press and stitch.

4 For the back, cut one length 208cm/82in. Turn in a hem at the bottom edge. Turn in a double hem at each side.

5 Make a paper pattern for the triangular sides. The longest vertical side of the triangle is 82in/208cm long. The horizontal, representing the bottom edge of the canopy is 214cm/84in wide. Draw a diagonal joining the two points. (The diagram below illustrates the point where the second piece of fabric is joined to the width of the first piece.)

6 Cut and piece the shape from fabric. Where two pieces of fabric join, sew together with a French seam so that no raw edges are visible.

7 Turn the pattern over for the opposite side.

8 At the bottom edge, turn in 0.75cm/¼in, press, then turn in another 3.75cm/1½in. Press and stitch. Turn in a double hem at each side.

9 One at a time, pin the diagonal edge of the side panels to the long edges of the front, right sides together.

10 Start at the top edge and stitch together to within 61cm/24in of the bottom edge.

11 Place the back and front right sides together, aligning top raw edges. Pin together.

12 Run a gathering thread through the top edge and pull up the threads to 100cm/40in wide.

MATERIALS

◆ *10m/11yd cotton voile 152cm/60in wide*

◆ *Sewing kit*

13 For the band to hold the tabs at the top of the net, cut two pieces of voile 4 x 41in/10 x 105cm.

14 Fold each in half lengthways, wrong sides together and press.

15 Align the raw edge of one band with the gathered raw edges of the canopy at the front. Slide the band down so that it sits 3.75cm/1½in below the gathered raw edges. Pin. Add the second band to the same position at the back. Baste the raw edges in place.

16 Stitch the top raw edge of the bands in place, stitching through all the layers at the same time.

17 Trim the excess fabric away from the top of the canopy to reduce the bulk behind the waistband.

18 To make the tabs to hang the net, cut five pieces 6.5 x 15cm/2½ x 6in.

19 Turn in the raw edges on each long edge and press.

20 Fold the tab in half lengthways, press, then stitch to hold. Fold in half across the width, press.

21 Position one tab at each end of the band, placing one raw edge at each side of the gathered raw edge. Pin.

22 Space the remaining tabs evenly across the band. Hold in place with a few basting stitches. Remove the pins.

23 Fold the band up over the raw edges of the tabs and the gathers and pin in place. Topstitch to hold.

24 Hold the canopy in place by sliding a length of cane through the tabs. The canopy should drape loosely over the sun lounger.

windbreak

◆

The windbreak can be made up of as many panels as you wish. If you choose a particularly heavy fabric, it is advisable to use a professional eyelet-punching service.

MATERIALS
- ◆ 1m/1yd of 137cm/54in wide navy
- ◆ 1m/1yd of 137cm/54in wide sky-blue
- ◆ 1m/1yd of 137cm/54in wide pink
- ◆ 1m/1yd of 137cm/54in wide green
- ◆ 32 eyelets 4cm/1 1/2in in diameter
- ◆ 5 bamboo poles

1 Trim each panel to 122cm/48in wide.

2 At the top and bottom of each panel, turn under 1.5cm/1/2in. Press. Turn under another 6.5cm/2 1/2in for the eyelet band. Press. Machine topstitch in place. (see picture next column)

3 Arrange the panels according to your preferred colour scheme. On alternate panels, at each side, turn under 1.5cm/1/2in to the wrong side. Press. On the remaining two panels, turn under 1.5cm/1/2in to the right side. Press.

4 Overlap the first panel with the second by 5cm/2in at one side, ensuring the overlap is sufficient to insert the poles and the raw edges are enclosed. Pin.

5 Double topstitch at each folded edge. Repeat to add the remaining panels.

6 At the outside edges, turn in 4cm/1 1/2in. Press and double topstitch to give a neat finish.

7 Insert the eyelets at evenly spaced intervals according to the manufacturer's instructions – four at the top and four at the bottom of each panel.

8 Insert the bamboo poles to finish.

deck chair

◆

If you are replacing a canvas, measure up the old decking and cut the new canvas to that measurement. If you have found an old frame, roughly estimate 1.3m/1½yd for a standard chair x the width of the seat.

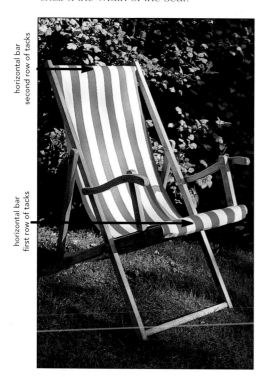

horizontal bar
second row of tacks

horizontal bar
first row of tacks

MATERIALS
◆ *1.3m/1½yd canvas*
◆ *Small round-headed tacks*
◆ *Hammer*
◆ *Glass paper*

1 Remove the old canvas. Clean the frame by sanding lightly or scrubbing with warm water and mild detergent.

2 If you have stripped away any paint finish, preserve the wood by lightly rubbing in teak oil with a soft cloth.

3 At each short end, turn under 2.5cm/1in. Press and turn under another 2.5cm/1in and press again.

4 Using five or six tacks fix one end of the canvas to the lower horizontal bar.

5 Wrap the canvas once around the bar to conceal the tacks.

6 Take the canvas over the top horizontal bar bringing the end to the front of the bar but concealed below the canvas.

7 Spacing the tacks evenly apart, secure the canvas in place. This is a little awkward and you may find it helpful if you have another pair of hands to hold up the canvas while you hammer in the tacks.

h a m m o c k

◆

Use the instructions below to make a new hammock or adapt or renovate an old one.

MATERIALS

◆ *3m/3yd of yellow and green canvas 137cm/54in wide*
◆ *20m/20yd of 1.5cm/½in wide rope*
◆ *Wooden batten 1m/1yd long with twelve evenly-spaced holes large enough to thread the rope through x 2*
◆ *Two steel rings 5–7.5cm/2–3in in diameter*
◆ *26 eyelets*
◆ *Sewing kit*

1 Square-up the fabric. Turn in 2cm/¾in across the width for the top and bottom. Press. Turn in another 5cm/2in and press. Double topstitch in place.

2 Repeat step 1 for turning in the sides.

3 Find the centre of the top and bottom seams and mark with a pin. This is the position of the centre eyelet.

4 Measure and mark with pins the position of six evenly-spaced eyelets to each side of the centre pin.
(see picture next column)

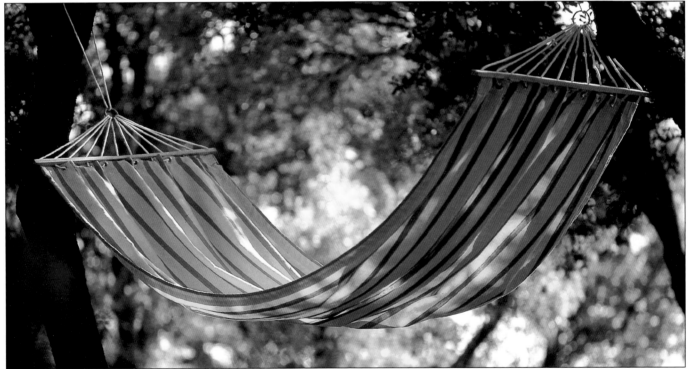

5 Insert the eyelets following the manufacturer's instructions. (*see figs 1–4 below*)

Fig 1

Fig 2

Fig 3

Fig 4

6 Thread a double thickness of rope through each side seam. Make a knotted loop at each end. (*see picture at bottom of column*)

7 With a third length of rope, leaving a long thread end, begin at the left-hand side of the wooden batten and thread through the loop then through the first hole at the left-hand side of the batten working from bottom to top.

8 Thread the rope through the metal ring above the centre of the batten, and then back through the second hole in the batten.

9 Thread the rope down through the first eyelet.

10 Thread through the next two eyelets, up through the batten to the ring and back. Repeat. (*see pic below*)

11 At the right-hand side thread the rope through the batten and knot the end around the loops at the end of the side seam. Repeat at the other end.

floor cushion

◆

Finished size: 66 x 66cm/26 x 26in

This cushion design can be adapted to fit any size cushion pad.

MATERIALS

- ◆ *1.6m/1¾yd blue*
- ◆ *46 x 46cm/18 x 18in white*
- ◆ *One skein each blue and white wool*
- ◆ *55cm/22in white zipper*
- ◆ *Sewing kit*

1 Cut two blue squares 70cm/27½in for the cushion front and back.

2 For the appliqué decoration, cut one white square 44.5 x 44.5cm/17½ x 17½in. Cut one blue square 19 x 19cm/7½ x 7½in.

3 Press under 2cm/¾in around the raw edge of each appliqué square. Trim the diagonal at each corner to reduce the bulk. Centre the small blue square on the white square. Pin, machine stitch close to the edge.
(see picture next column)

4 Decorate the edge with blanket stitch.

5 Repeat to stitch the white square to the cushion front.

6 To insert the zipper, pin and baste the cushion front and back right sides together along one edge. Measure and mark the centred zipper position. Machine stitch the cushion front and back together at each side of the zipper position taking a 2cm/¾in seam.
(see picture next column)

7 Press the seam open. On the seam, position the zipper right side down over the basted area. Pin. Using a zipper foot, stitch the zipper in position, without catching the teeth of the zipper.

8 Open the zipper slightly. Stitch the cushion front to the cushion back using a 2cm/¾in seam and rounding the corners. Overcast the raw edges.

beach bag and mat

◆

BEACH BAG

Finished size: 33cm/13in diameter 74cm/29in long

Seersucker is an ideal choice for this beach-side ensemble. The bag is a drawstring tube that neatly stows the mat for carrying. Add a small pocket on the inside to house valuables.

MATERIALS

- ◆ *1m/1yd of 112cm/44in-wide blue seersucker for the base and bag top*
- ◆ *112 x 76cm/44 x 30in green check seersucker for the bag body*
- ◆ *Green cord for the handle*
- ◆ *Paper for template*
- ◆ *Sewing kit*

1 Make a paper template of a 35.75cm/ 14in diameter circle for the bag base. Cut one from blue fabric. For the bag top, cut one piece 44 x 112cm/ 17 x 44in from blue.

2 Stitch the bag top to the green check, along the 112cm/44in edge. Press the seam open. Turn in a double hem at the 112cm/44in raw edge of the blue and baste.

3 Fold and pin the fabric in half length-ways, right sides together. On the blue seam line, measure and mark points 15cm and 18cm/6in and 7in from the seam joining the green check. The 3cm/1in gap marks the point where the cord handle will be threaded through.

4 Beginning 3cm/1in from the basted double hem of the blue, stitch the side seam, reinforcing the stitching at each side of the 3cm/1in gap.

5 At the top of the tube, turn down 12.75cm/5in to the wrong side, so that the open seam at the top of the bag aligns with the gap in the side seam. Press and pin. Mark the channel for the cord handle.

6 Stitch the edge of the channel closest to the top of the bag, so that the stitching clears the channel. Reinforce the stitching at the top of the gap.

7 Place the cord close to the stitched line. Anchor in place, then stitch the fabric together, enclosing the cord in the channel.

8 With right sides together, fit the bag base to the tube. Pin and stitch.

BEACH MAT COVER

Tailor-made to fit a length of foam, this simple idea can be adapted for any size and thickness of mat. The cover can be easily removed for washing.

MATERIALS

◆ *Green and blue check seersucker – 4m/4yd*

◆ *Scraps of blue for the ties*

◆ *Foam – 1.8m x 80 x 3.5cm deep/70 x 32 x 1½in deep*

● Use 1.5cm/½in seam allowances unless otherwise stated.

1 For the ties, cut four lengths 5 x 30.5cm/2 x 12in. Turn in 0.75cm/¼in seam at each short edge. Press. Turn in 0.75cm/¼in along each long edge. Press. Fold the tie in half lengthways, wrong sides together. Press. Machine topstitch around the folded edges.

2 For the mat top and bottom, cut two pieces of fabric the length and width of the foam plus seam allowances.

3 From the remainder, for the envelope-style flap, cut one piece the width of the mat plus seam allowances x 30.5cm/ 12in long.

4 For the sides, measure the thickness of the foam, and cut two pieces the length of the foam x the thickness, plus seam allowances. Cut two pieces the width of the foam x the thickness plus seam allowances.

5 Join a long length to each side of one short length. Press the seams open. Put the remaining short length to one side.

6 Pin the length for the sides to the beachmat top, right sides together.

7 Align raw edges and begin stitching down one long edge. Stop stitching 1.5cm/½in from the corner. Lift the machine foot.

8 Fold the side strip up at 45° angle away from the quilt, then bring it back down to align with the next side.

9 The movement will create a pleat at the corner, allowing sufficient fabric to create a mitre.

10 Continue stitching around the three sides.

11 When you return to the top, turn in 1.5cm/½in across the raw edge and press.

12 Pin two ties 7.5cm/3in from each seam joining the side to the top. Stitch the turning. Put aside.

13 Turn in a small seam at each short end of the remaining side strip.

14 Centre the strip along one short edge of the bottom panel of the beach mat. Stitch the two together. Put aside.

15 Turn in and stitch a seam allowance around three sides of the envelope flap, leaving one long edge free.

16 Align the raw edge of the envelope flap with that of the side strip at the short end of the bottom panel. Pin.
(see picture next column)

17 Between the bottom panel and the envelope flap, place the ties 7.5cm/3in from each raw edge. Stitch together.

18 With right sides together, pin the two halves of the beach mat together.

19 Machine stitch the two sides together. Turn right side out to finish and insert the foam mat.

20 If you choose, use the ties for decoration only and slipstitch the green check seersucker closed at the top edge.

garden candles

◆

Candle making has become such a popular activity that you should be able to find most of the necessary materials at your local art and craft stores. There are specialist candle making suppliers that offer a mail order service.

MATERIALS

- ◆ *Candle making wax*
- ◆ *Microsoft or beeswax*
- ◆ *Nylon wicks*
- ◆ *Sustainers*
- ◆ *Slugs (weight)*
- ◆ *Pencil (or thin rod will do)*
- ◆ *Thin knitting needle or similar*
- ◆ *Containers*
- ◆ *Old saucepans*
- ◆ *Pliers*

1 Collect all your materials together. Protect your work surfaces with newspaper.

2 Heat up your glass containers by standing them in a tray of warm water then place in the oven at the lowest temperature setting. Leave until ready to fill with the melted wax. Ensure that the inside of the container does not get wet.

3 Melt wax and Microsoft slowly in a saucepan. Do not put the saucepan directly on the heat source. Use a double boiler or place the saucepan in a larger container, as shown.

4 Cut a length of wick the depth of your container plus approximately 5cm/2in extra for tying on the sustainer and slug and winding around the rod.

5 Attach a sustainer to one end of the wick and fix in place by crimping the neck with a pair of long-nosed pliers.

6 Thread on the slug so that it sits on top of the sustainer. The weight will help keep the wick in the correct position.

7 When the wax has melted, allow it to cool to approximately 70°C. Add any fragrances or insect repellents at this point and stir in gently.

8 Holding the wick so that it hangs just above the bottom of the container pour the melted wax in to the warm container.

9 Wind the end of the wick around a thin rod or pencil.

10 As the wax cools it shrinks in the middle, making a well. To prevent this from happening, prick the centre every 10 minutes until set. After approximately an hour, top up with melted wax.

11 When the wax is hard, trim the wick.

hessian tote bag

◆

Finished size: 48.25 x 28cm/19 x 11in

This practical tote bag, made of hessian and ticking, will withstand the wear and tear of outdoor life.

MATERIALS

- ◆ 30cm/12in hessian
- ◆ 30cm/12in green and white ticking
- ◆ 1.6m/1¾yd tape for the handles
- ◆ Sewing kit

● Use 1.5cm/½in seams throughout.

1 Cut the ticking into two equal size pieces and square up the edges.

2 Square up the hessian length and overcast the raw edges to stop the threads from fraying.

3 With right sides together, align the 30cm/12in raw edge of ticking with one short edge of hessian. Stitch the two together. Repeat at the other end of the hessian. Press without distorting the hessian. (*see pic at top of next column*)

4 Refold the hessian in half across the width, right sides together and pin the side seams. Machine stitch the seams, reinforcing the stitching across the seams joining the hessian to the ticking.

5 Turn the bag right side out. Press.

6 At the remaining raw edge of the ticking turn in a small hem and press. On the right side of the fabric, stitch the folded edges of the ticking together to form the lining bag bottom.

7 Push the lining into the hessian bag. Turn back 7.5cm/3in of ticking to show on the hessian side of the bag.

8 Cut the handle tape in half. Turn under the raw edges and press. Pin the handles in position and stitch through all the fabric layers, reinforcing the tape ends with a square of stitching.

lavender flower box

◆

This is a seasonal project that can be replaced each year. Try other aromatic cuttings such as sage, thyme, rosemary and marjoram. If you do not have enough of one variety, use different stems in combination.

MATERIALS

- ◆ *A plastic or terracotta window box*
- ◆ *Garden wire*
- ◆ *Pliers*
- ◆ *Large quantity of fresh lavender*
- ◆ *Florists' scissors*
- ◆ *Heavy duty polythene for the flower box liner*

1 Wind lengths of garden wire in parallel horizontal bands around your base window box. Secure each length by twisting the ends around each other. Do not make the bands too tight or you will find it impossible to thread the lavender. *(see picture next column)*

2 Repeat to make vertical bands by centring each length under the base of the window box and weaving the remaining sections through the horizontal bands to make a grid.

3 Using the longest stalks, thread the lavender vertically through the grid all around the box. *(see picture next column)*

4 Repeat, weaving the stalks horizontally until you have a close weave.

5 Trim the vertical stalks flush with the top edge of the box.

6 Use the trimmed stalks to fill any gaps.

7 Gently ease the woven lavender away from the base.

8 Line with heavy duty plastic and make some drainage holes in the base. Put the lavender box in position in your garden before filling with potting compost and planting up.

p e b b l e   p a v i n g   s t o n e s

◆

Finished size: 38 x 38cm/15 x 15in

From the picture below you can see how easy it is to create a paving stone design. Use rubber gloves when handling cement.

MATERIALS

◆ *Length of wood 2.5cm/1in thick and sufficiently long to make a frame for four sides of the tile*
◆ *A wooden length to use as a straight edge*
◆ *Hammer and nails*
◆ *Selection of pebbles*
◆ *Sand and cement*

1 Cut four lengths of wood for the frame and fix the pieces together.

2 On a flat surface, arrange the pebbles as required in the base of the frame. Remove the pebbles.

3 Following the manufacturer's instructions, make up a mix of concrete. Pour into the frame.

4 Drag a length of wood across the surface of the wet concrete, so that it is flat. Remove any excess, or fill in any dips in the surface and level again in the same way.

5 Add the pebbles to the surface in the required arrangement. Allow the concrete to dry.

6 Tap the wooden frame to release the paving stone.

buttoned tablemats

◆

Finished size: 43.25 x 33cm/17 x 13in

These easy-to-make pastel-coloured mats are finished with attractive shell buttons and make a beautiful summer table setting.

MATERIALS

◆ *46 x 36cm/18 x 14in narrow blue stripe*
◆ *30 x 23cm/11½ x 9in wide blue stripe*
◆ *4 shell buttons*
◆ *Sewing kit*

1 Turn in and press 0.75cm/¼in along each raw edge of the narrow blue stripe fabric. Turn in another 0.75cm/¼in and press. Machine stitch to hold.

2 Repeat with the wide blue stripe decorative rectangle.

3 Centre the decorative rectangle on the tablemat. Pin.

4 Position a button at each corner and hand stitch in place through all the layers. Remove the pins.

beaded tablerunners

◆

Finished size: 50.75 x 151.25cm/20 x 59½in

On this simple pair of runners I have made a feature of the seams, bringing the turning to the right side.

MATERIALS

To make one runner:

◆ *57 x 157.5cm/22½ x 62in*
natural-coloured linen
◆ *A selection of carved wooden beads*
◆ *Linen thread*
◆ *Sewing kit*

1 Turn in 0.75cm/¼in all around the linen edge. Press. Turn in another 2.5cm/1in. Press. Unfold the turnings.

2 Turn in each corner. Clip the fabric at a diagonal to reduce the bulk, leaving a small seam allowance.
(see picture next column)

3 On a remnant of fabric, fray the threads and pull away several lengths on which to thread the beads.

4 Knot one bead onto the end of a 15cm/6in length of thread.

5 String several beads and make a knot in the thread to hold them in place. To leave a gap, make a large knot and continue threading beads.

6 Stitch the lengths of beaded thread at equal intervals to the second foldline and make a knot so that the thread end will be caught in the seam.

7 Refold the tablerunner seams and hand stitch the mitre.

8 Machine stitch the seam in place 2cm/¾in from the folded edge.

two-coloured tablecloth

◆

Adapt the measurements to fit your own round table

A stylish, lined circular tablecloth with four slits from the floor to the table top.

MATERIALS

- ◆ 5.5m/6yd main colour
- ◆ 2m/2⅛yd contrast
- ◆ 5m/5½yd lining
- ◆ Paper to make a pattern
- ◆ Chalk marker

- ◆ Sewing kit

1 Cut the main colour in half across the width. Join the pieces together along one long edge. Press the seam open. (see picture next page, column 1)

2 Fold the fabric into quarters, right sides together.

3 Measure the diameter of the table, add on twice the height of the tablecloth plus 10cm/4in for seams.

4 Make a paper pattern for a quarter of the tablecloth. Round one corner.

5 For the pattern for the contrast band, draw another arc inside the first, 22cm/9in away. Cut the pieces.

6 Pin the main colour pattern to the fabric and carefully cut out the circle.

7 The contrast border is cut on the bias and is pieced together.

8 Cut the pattern for the contrast band into sections small enough to fit the width of your fabric. It may help to cut more than one pattern from paper.

9 Place the pattern at one end of the fabric. Using a fabric marker, lightly draw around the pattern piece.

10 Fill the fabric with the required number of sections, remembering to leave a seam allowance all around each for joining the sections together.

11 Cut out each piece adding the seam allowance by eye as you cut.

12 Piece the sections of contrast fabric together until you have a complete circle for the hem.

13 Press the seams out flat. Try the fit of the contrast band and adapt the seams where necessary

14 Turn in a seam allowance around the raw edge of the main colour. Pin to the contrast band. Topstitch in place.

15 Turn in a seam allowance around the raw edge of the contrast band. Press.

16 Place the cloth over the table and with a chalk marker and a straight edge, mark the position of the slits.

17 Spread the cloth on a flat surface and cut the slits following the marked line.

18 Turn the raw edges a scant 0.5cm/ ⅛in to the wrong side of the cloth and fingerpress, then slipstitch in place.

19 If your table is adapted to take a parasol, cut a small circle in the centre of the tablecloth, large enough to post the parasol pole through. Turn under a small seam allowance and press.

20 Cut and piece the lining to fit the tablecloth.

21 Turn in a small seam at the raw edges at the centre of the lining and outer edges. Pin the lining to the cloth.

22 Slipstitch the lining in place.

patchwork picnic cloth

◆

Finished size: 155 x 132cm/61 x 52in

Patchwork at its simplest, this is a fast and easy project for you to make – made using cotton sheeting.

MATERIALS
106 ◀
- ◆ *2m/2yd lime green*
- ◆ *1m/1yd orange*
- ◆ *1m/1yd pink*
- ◆ *1.6m/1¾yd of 137cm/54in-wide calico for backing*
- ◆ *Thick navy thread*
- ◆ *Sewing kit*
- ◆ *Pencil and ruler*

1 Cut six pink and six orange rectangles 24 x 39.5cm/9½ x 15½in – twelve in total.

2 For the border, cut two lime green strips 165 x 26.75cm/65 x 10½in and two borders 142.25 x 26.75cm/56 x 10½in.

3 On a clean, flat surface, arrange the pink and orange rectangles, four wide and three deep, alternating the colour-ways throughout.

4 Using 0.75cm/¼in seam allowance, stitch the rectangles into the three rows.

5 Stitch the three rows together.

6 Along one long edge of each border, find and mark with a pin the centre point. Find the centre of each side of the cloth and match the two points. With right sides together pin each border to the cloth, allowing the excess to overlap at each edge.

7 Stitch each border in place. Begin stitching 0.75cm/¼in from the raw edge of the cloth.

8 To mitre the corners, press under the 0.75cm/¼in seam allowance on the inside raw edge of each border.

9 Fold the cloth diagonally at each corner and, with a pencil and ruler, draw a diagonal line at an accurate 45° angle. Baste along the line, then open out the cloth and check the mitre lies flat. Adjust as necessary.

10 Machine stitch the mitre. Trim away the excess border.

11 The border is 20cm/8in wide. Turn in the excess and press. Fold in a diagonal at each corner across the point where the two pressed lines cross. Trim away the corners, leaving a small seam. Refold the seams and stitch the mitre.

12 With navy thread, sew the running stitch decoration. Cut the backing 1.5cm/½in smaller than the cloth. Turn in a seam and press. Slipstitch the backing in place.

envelope cushion covers

◆

Finished size: 46 x 49cm/18 x 19¼ in

The envelope cushion cover is a novel and extremely economical way of using 100 percent linen tea towels.

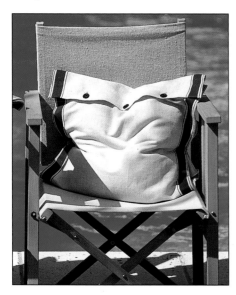

MATERIALS
◆ *Two purchased tea towels*
◆ *2.5m/2¾yd of 3cm/1¼in-wide tape for the button band*
◆ *5 buttons 2cm/¾in diameter*
◆ *Sewing kit*

● Use 0.75cm/¼in seam throughout.

1 Turn in a hem around each edge of the tea towels, press and machine stitch in place.

2 Stitch two towels together at one short edge. Press the seam open.

3 Cut the button-band tape in half. Machine stitch tape along the long edges of the wrong side of the cushion so that it covers the turned-in edge. Trim away any excess.

4 At one short end turn in 5cm/2in and press. Stitch in place close to the folded-down edge.

5 Make three evenly-spaced buttonholes along this edge.

6 At the opposite short edge, turn down 7.5cm/3in. Press and stitch. Sew on three buttons to correspond with the buttonholes.

7 Half way down the right and left-hand side of the button band make one buttonhole.

8 Stitch on two buttons to correspond with the buttonholes.

director's chair loose cover

◆

Follow the directions below to make a cover for your director's chair. The directions can be adapted to suit other chair variations.

MATERIALS

◆ *Pink, orange and purple madras check*

◆ *16 eyelets each 1in/2.5cm in diameter*

◆ *Large sheets of paper*

◆ *Sewing kit*

1 Measure the height and width of the front of the chairback. Add on the thickness of the chair sides and top (A).

2 Measure the depth and width of the seat (B). Add 12cm/4½in to the depth.

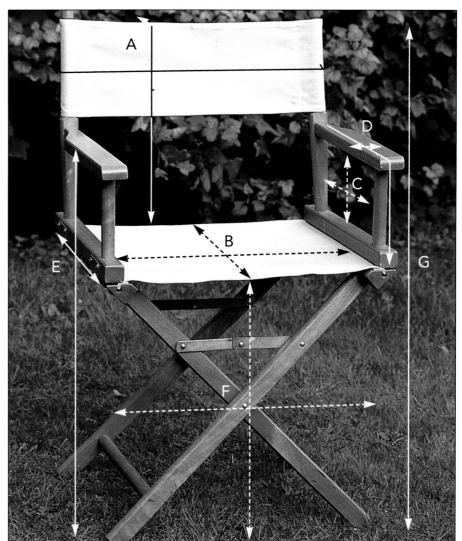

3 Measure the width and drop from the top of the arm to the seat (C);
● the width of the arm and the length from the back to the chair (D); and

● the width and drop from the top of the arm to the floor (E). To the width of E add 13cm/5in. Double the fabric quantity for C, D and E – one set for each side.

4 Measure the width of the chair and the drop from the front of the seat to the floor (F), then measure the back of the chair from the top to the floor (G). To the width of F and G add 13cm/5in.

5 To all your measurements add a generous 1.5cm/½in seam all around, except for hem edges of E, F and G. Add 10cm/4in hem.

6 With the patterns, make a mock-up to ensure a good fit without straining the seams.

7 Cut each pattern from fabric.

8 Cut eight ties 35 x 8cm/14 x 3¼in.

9 Centre the base of A to the back of B. Make a pleat 6cm/2¼in deep in B, parallel to A. Sew the pleat, then keep the pleat free during assembly.

10 Sew D to the top and front edge of C. Stitch to within a seam allowance width of the corner of C. Lift the presser foot. Rotate, then realign D and stitch the second side in place.

11 Try the fit over the arm. Make another in reverse.

12 Stitch the lower edge of C to B. Sew the vertical of C to the cut-out edge of A. Sew the end of D to the top of the cut-out (it does not complete the cut-out). Repeat at both sides.

13 Press in a double 3cm/1¼in seam at both sides of E, F and G. Unfold the hems and keep clear of the stitching. Sew the top of E across the cut-out on A, along D and down the front edge of D. Repeat on the other arm. Centre F to

B and sew, continuing across the lower ends of D.

14 Centre the top of G to A and sew. With the hem edges of E and G level, sew G to E and A at the sides from a point level with seam B–F on the front upwards.

15 To make the fabric fit at the top of the chair, on each side seam, to align with the top seam, form a triangle shape. Stitch across the triangle at right angles 2cm/1in from the point. Test the fit.

16 Sew the pressed hems on the sides of the openings. Press a 5cm/2in double hem on all lower edges.

17 Add eyelets through the hems following the instructions for the *Hammock*.

18 Sew the ties, following the instructions for the *Covered Chair Seat*.

covered chairback and seat

◆

This chairback cover is quite simply a padded rectangle which folds in half over the chairback. The idea can be adapted for most chairs.

MATERIALS

- ◆ *Orange cotton and linen union*
- ◆ *Yellow cotton and linen union*
- ◆ *Wadding*
- ◆ *Sewing kit*

1 For ties, from yellow, cut eight strips 6.5 x 40.75cm/2½ x 16in. Cut four from orange. Press in a seam at the short ends. Press in 1.5cm/½in along each long edge. Fold in half lengthways and press. Stitch around the ties.

2 Make a paper template of the chair seat. Cut two from fabric ¾in/2cm larger all around. Cut one shape from wadding slightly smaller than the template.

3 Position four ties on the right side of the back edge of each cushion 5–7.5cm/2–3in from the sides. Pin. Centre the wadding on the wrong side of the cushion front. Baste together.

4 Place the back and front, right sides together and pin. Begin stitching 10cm/4in from one corner of the back of the cushion, catching the ties in the stitching. Leave a gap at the centre back.

5 Turn the cushion right side out through the gap. Hand stitch the gap.

6 Make a template of the shape of both sides of the chairback. Cut one shape, from orange for the wrong side, adding 2cm/¾in all around. Cut one shape from wadding slightly smaller than the template. For the cushion front divide the template into four. Cut two sections from orange and two from yellow adding 2cm/¾in seams all around.

7 Stitch together the orange and yellow pieces to form the cushion front.

8 Make up the cushion following the instructions at steps 3–5. Insert the ties at convenient points at each side of the cushion and tie each around the sides of the chair.

folding picnic stool

◆

Made for a stool with a centre-side opening. If replacing a worn out seat use the old cover as your template.

Adapt the measurements to fit your own stool

MATERIALS

- ◆ *Red and orange striped fabric*
- ◆ *Sewing kit*
- ◆ *Stool frame*
- ◆ *Silver galvanised paint*

1 Using silver galvanised paint, paint the framework of a stool.

2 Determine the width and depth of the chair seat required. Add to your measurement 2.5cm/1in to the front and back for turnings. Add 10cm/4in to each side. Cut the fabric to your requirements.

3 At the front and back, turn under 1.5cm/½in, then another 1.5cm/½in. Press and stitch to hold.

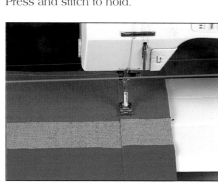

4 At each side turn under 3cm/1¼in. Press. Machine stitch to hold. Turn under another 6.5cm/2½in and machine stitch close to the folded edge, leaving maximum room for the bars of the stool.

index